# 5 Cleanliness … n

*A Collection of Quranic Verses and S… …een*



Islām places great significance on cleanliness. However, in addition to external cleanliness, it is also good to remain clean internally and ritually. A human being should always try to remain in a state of cleanliness, spiritual purity, and tahaarah (ritual purity). When we attain purity in all three areas, we have fulfilled our prerequisites and are ready to worship Allāh in the rightful manner.

# Lesson 1

## USE PURE WATER FOR CLEANING

وَ أَنْزَلْنَا مِنَ السَّمَاءِ مَاءً طَهُوراً

And We sent down from the sky purifying water.

Sūrah al-Furqān, Verse 48

Imam Ali (a) loved inviting people to his house and sharing meals with them. One day, he invited a friend and his son over for dinner. They were both so excited to visit the Imam and share a meal with him! After all, the Imam (a) was a cheerful and loving person, and he always showed extra kindness to his guests.

When they finished eating, the Imam (a) brought a jug of water and clean towel so that he could wash his guest's hands. Shocked, the man asked, "how can you wash my hands? You are my Imam and leader!" The man could not believe that Imam Ali (a), with all his greatness, was doing something that servants would normally be doing.

The Imam (a) replied, "You are my guest, and I would like the honor of serving you because this is what Allah likes. Please wash your hands carefully and don't feel embarrassed."

The Imam (a) then told his own son who was sitting next to him to wash the other boy's hands.

The two guests felt very touched by this act of kindness and left the Imam's home feeling humbled.

Biḥār ul-Anwār, Vol. 9, P. 598

اِغْسِلُوا أَيْدِيَكُمْ قَبْلَ الطَّعَامِ وَ بَعْدَهُ

**Imam Ja'far as-Sadiq (a):**
Wash your hands before and after you eat.

Mashāim, Vol. 2, #1594

# Lesson 2

## BE CLEAN & PRESENTABLE

وَ اللّٰهُ يُحِبُّ الْمُطَّهِّرِيْنَ

And Allah loves those who stay pure.

Sūrah at-Tawbah, Verse 108

One day, a friend of the Prophet (s) was coming over to his house. Knowing this, the Prophet (s) dressed up, washed his face, combed his hair, and put on some fragrance.

He had a habit of always being clean and smelling nice.

When his wife saw how he took the time and effort to prepare for his guest, she asked, "why did you do all of that?"

He replied to her, "Allah loves for us to look neat and clean when meeting our friends."

Makārim al-Akhlāq, P. 51

خُذُوا مِنْ شُعُورِكُمْ وَ اسْتَاكُوا وَ تَزَيَّنُوا

**Prophet Muhammad (s):**
Take care of your hair, brush your teeth, and beautify yourselves.

Kanz ul-ʿUmmāl, Vol. 6, P. 640

# Lesson 3

## WEAR CLEAN CLOTHES

وَ ثِيَابَكَ فَطَهِّرْ

And purify your clothes.

Sūrah al-Muddathir, Verse 4

The Prophet (s) cared a lot about being clean and always smelling good. One day, he saw a pile of laundry lying around his home, so he began to wash the clothes.

Moments later, his wife came up to him and offered, "O Prophet, let me wash them!" He was very happy with her offer and accepted her help.

As they washed the clothes together, he taught her, "everything, even clothes, praise Allah (by doing dhikr)," he said. "But when clothes become dirty, all of that stops."

Mizān al-Ḥikmah, Vol. 10, P. 940

اِغْسِلُوا ثِيَابَكُمْ وَ تَنَظَّفُوا

**Prophet Muhammad (s):**
Wash your clothes and be clean.

Kanz ul-ʿUmmāl, Vol. 6, P. 640

## Lesson 4

### EAT PURE FOOD

فَلْيَنْظُرْ اَيُّهَا اَزْكَىٰ طَعَاماً

Let him find out which of them has the purest food.

Sūrah al-Kahf, Verse 19

Many years ago, in the city of Rome, it was illegal to worship Allah, the One. If anyone believed and worshipped one God, the evil king would torture and even kill them.

There was one group of young people who wanted to worship Allah freely, so they escaped from the city and hid inside a cave. The king's army searched for them everywhere, but Allah protected them by sealing the cave with a huge boulder. Then, Allah allowed them to sleep for many, many years — 300 years to be exact! This is why they are now known as The People of the Cave (*Ashaabul Kahf*).

In Surah al-Kahf, Allah says that when He finally woke them up from their sleep, they had no idea how long they had been sleeping. They thought they might have been asleep for a few hours or maybe even a full day. The only thing they knew for sure was that they felt very hungry! Even though they thought it was risky to leave, they decided that one of them would go back to the city to buy some food for everyone. Before leaving, one of them advised him, "And be sure to buy food from a clean and pure place."

Even though they had not eaten for 300 years, The People of the Cave still made sure that the food they ate was pure and halaal.

Tafsīr an-Namūnah

مِنْ اَخْلَاقِ الْأَنْبِيَاءِ التَّنَظُّفُ

**Imam Ali ar-Ridha (a):**
It is from the manners (akhlaq) of the Prophets to be clean.

Muntakhab Mizān al-Ḥikmah, #6167

# Lesson 5

## KEEP THE CITY CLEAN

بَلْدَةٌ طَيِّبَةٌ

A clean, pure city.

Sūrah Saba', Verse 15

It was a sunny day in the city of Medina when the fourth Imam, Imam Sajjad (a), was walking through town with some friends. As they were passing through one of the streets, they noticed that it was quite dirty; there were rocks and rubble everywhere!

Without saying a word, the Imam (a) gently got off his horse and bent down to gather the rocks with his blessed hands.

His friends looked surprised, wondering why he would stop in the middle of the street. One of them finally asked, "may my mother and father be sacrificed for you*! What are you doing?"

The Imam (a) turned toward his friends and said, "These rocks are in the middle of the way, and someone might get hurt."

After hearing this, the men immediately came down from their horses to help the Imam (a) clean the streets. As they pushed aside the rocks, they thought about how blessed they were to spend time with the Imam (a). He was always inspiring them to do good and help others.

Biḥār ul-Anwār, Vol. 75, P. 160

*In our ahadith and du'as, when someone wants to show the highest level of loyalty and love toward another person, they use this expression.

أُكْنُسُوا أَفْنِيَتَكُمْ

**Prophet Muhammad (s):**
Sweep the front of your houses.

Nahj ul-Faṣāḥah, P. 296

# Quiz Time!

1. Imam Sadiq (a) advises us to __________ before and after eating.
a. say bismillah
b. wash our hands
c. do wudhu

2. In verse 108 of Surah at-Tawbah, we learn that Allah loves those who are always _________.
a. pure
b. nice
c. honest

3. Why did the Prophet (s) say that it was so important to clean dirty clothes?
a. Because everything, even clothes, recite Allah's dhikr.
b. Because being clean makes you look nice in front of other people.
c. Because after a while, you might get annoyed by the smell of dirty clothes.

4. When the People of the Cave woke up from their deep sleep and decided to search for food, they made sure to find food that was _____________.
a. delicious
b. vegetarian
c. pure

5. What does the Prophet (s) advise us to do in front of our homes?
a. Wait outside to invite strangers in
b. Plant a garden with fruits and flowers
c. Sweep and clean the area

6. Name three things that you can do on a daily basis to stay clean.

Email your answers to QUIZZES@KISAKIDS.ORG, and we will send you a certificate!